Common Core Lesso
History of tl

By Carole Marsh
Published by Gallopade International, Inc.

Printed in the U.S.A. (Peachtree City, Georgia)

TABLE OF CONTENTS

G: Includes Graphic Organizer
GO: Graphic Organizer is also available 8½" x 11" online download at www.gallopade.com/client/go
(numbers above correspond to the graphic organizer numbers online)

What Is Geology?

Read the text and answer the questions.

The Earth is very old—more than four billion years old!—and has been changing constantly since it first formed. The study of the Earth and its processes is called geology. Geologists study what the Earth is made of, how it is put together, and how it has changed over time.

Clues to the Earth's history can be found in the rocks and formations that make up the Earth. If you could peel away the layers of the Earth, you would see much of our planet's history from long ago to today. Geologists read these layers like pages in a book. The age of the rocks tells us about what the Earth looked like long ago. Plant and animal fossils found in the Earth's crust tell us about what life forms lived long ago.

Geologists also study the Earth processes such as weathering, erosion, and volcanic activity. Earth processes that occur today have been affecting the Earth throughout its history. Geologists study these processes to better understand how the Earth has changed over long periods of time. Geologists use the clues hidden in the Earth's rocky layers to piece together what they know about the history of the Earth.

1. Match each of the following questions to whether they are best answered by paragraph 1, 2, or 3 of the text.
   A. _____ Why do geologists study processes that change the Earth?
   B. _____ What is the purpose of studying the Earth's layers?
   C. _____ What is geology?
2. The suffix "-logy" means "the study of."
   A. Infer the meaning of the prefix "geo-".
   B What does a geologist do?
3. What clues in the Earth help us understand what the Earth looked like long ago?
4. What is the relationship between geology and the history of the Earth?
5. Explain what is meant by the comparison: "Geologists read these layers like pages in a book."

CONCEPTS & PROCESSES

What Is Inside the Earth?

Read the text and answer the questions.

To understand the history of the Earth, geologists first must understand what is inside the Earth. There are many important geologic processes that begin inside the Earth. But, what does the inside of the Earth look like?

Since geologists cannot travel deep into the Earth to collect rock samples, they use geological evidence from the surface of the Earth (rocks, layer patterns, etc.) to construct a model of the Earth's layers. A model is a tool that scientists use to show and study things that cannot be easily seen, like a molecule or the solar system. A model is what a scientist *thinks* something looks like. Models can take many forms: drawings, constructions (like mobiles or globes), and comparisons or analogies.

Scientists believe that the Earth has many layers. Most of the rocks and fossils that geologists study come from the outer layer of the Earth, called the crust. Below the crust lies a very thick layer called the mantle. The mantle is divided into two parts. The upper mantle is solid rock, while the rest is partly liquid rock. The center layer of the Earth is called the core. The outer core is liquid metal while the inner core is solid metal.

1. A. Which definition below matches the meaning of the word model as it is used in the text?

a)	noun;	person hired to wear and display clothing
b)	noun;	a simple diagram or description used to explain something
c)	noun;	highly respected person worthy of being followed

B. What is the reason for creating a model?

2. Identify each layer of the Earth:
   _____ inner core
   _____ outer core
   _____ crust
   _____ upper mantle
   _____ mantle

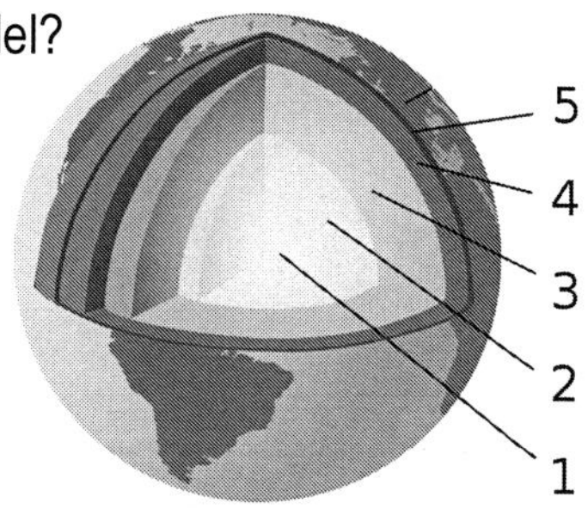

3. Why is the crust important for studying the history of the Earth?

Slow & Fast Changes

Read the text and answer the questions.

Since the beginning, the Earth has experienced many changes. Some of the changes are hard to see since they happen slowly over many thousands of years. Other process happen quickly and can often be seen or felt.

Slow Changes

Weathering is the breaking down of rocks or minerals caused by ice, roots, and natural chemicals. The rocks or minerals are broken down into smaller pieces. For example, when water fills a crack in a rock and freezes, it expands, splitting the rock apart.

Erosion is the gradual wearing away of soil, rock, or land by wind, water or other natural forces. This process usually involves a grinding or rubbing motion. Water in a river washes against its rocky bed. The water's movement might not seem like much, but moving water can eventually carve canyons out of the rocky Earth.

Erosion causes rocks to break into smaller and smaller pieces. Wind, water, and even glacial movements often carry away pieces of rock, soil, and sand. When these tiny pieces of earth are deposited in another location, it is called deposition. Deposition is a process that can cause deltas to form at the mouth of a river, or sandy beaches to form near the coast.

Fast Changes

While some of the processes that affect the Earth occur over many years, others happen rapidly and make dramatic changes. Fast changes occur when energy builds up and is suddenly released. Examples of fast changes include earthquakes, landslides, and volcanoes.

An earthquake is a sudden, violent rolling or shaking of the ground. Earthquakes are caused by pressure that builds up as the Earth's tectonic plates shift. A volcano is a mountain that erupts and spews out rocks, gas, and lava. Volcanoes usually form along faults, where magma from the upper mantle works its way to the crust. A landslide occurs when soil, rocks, pebbles, and boulders suddenly slide down a slope at one time. Landslides normally happen when a slope becomes unstable. Erosion, weathering, and heavy rains can all contribute to landslides.

PART A: Use the text to answer the questions.

1. A. Describe the effects of weathering and erosion.
   B. How are they similar? How are they different?

2. A. Describe the process of deposition.
   B. What has to happen first before deposition can occur?

Number the events below in the correct order of sequence

_____ Near the ocean, the soil settles at the river's mouth.
_____ The soil creates a raised fan-shaped landform called a delta.
_____ The rushing river carries the soil toward the ocean.
_____ The soil collects at the river's mouth year after year.
_____ Rainwater washes soil into a nearby river.

4. Explain how deposition helps to create new formations on the Earth's surface.

5. Make inferences from the text to describe the effects of each fast change on the Earth's surface.
   A. volcanic eruption B. landslide C. earthquake

6. Infer how people might tell if an earthquake, volcanic eruption, or landslide is coming.

PART B: Read the text and answer the questions.

Geologists examine the changes that occur in modern times to understand how the Earth has changed in the past. The idea that geological changes happened the same way in the ancient past as they do today is called the Uniformitarian Principle.

Geologists study both slow and fast changes because they are connected. Slow changes, like erosion and weathering, can cause fast changes like landslides and earthquakes. Each movement of the Earth's crust is a clue to understanding how the Earth changes.

"The present is the key to the past." —Archibald Geikie

7. A. Define the Uniformitarian Principle.
   B. How does it help geologists understand the history of the Earth?

8. How does the quotation by Archibald Geikie relate to the information in the texts?

9. Explain how the Uniformitarian Principle supports Archibald Geikie's point of view.

Comparing Changes

Complete the Venn diagram by comparing and contrasting slow and fast changes to the Earth. Compare each in terms of effect on the Earth and role in the Earth's history.

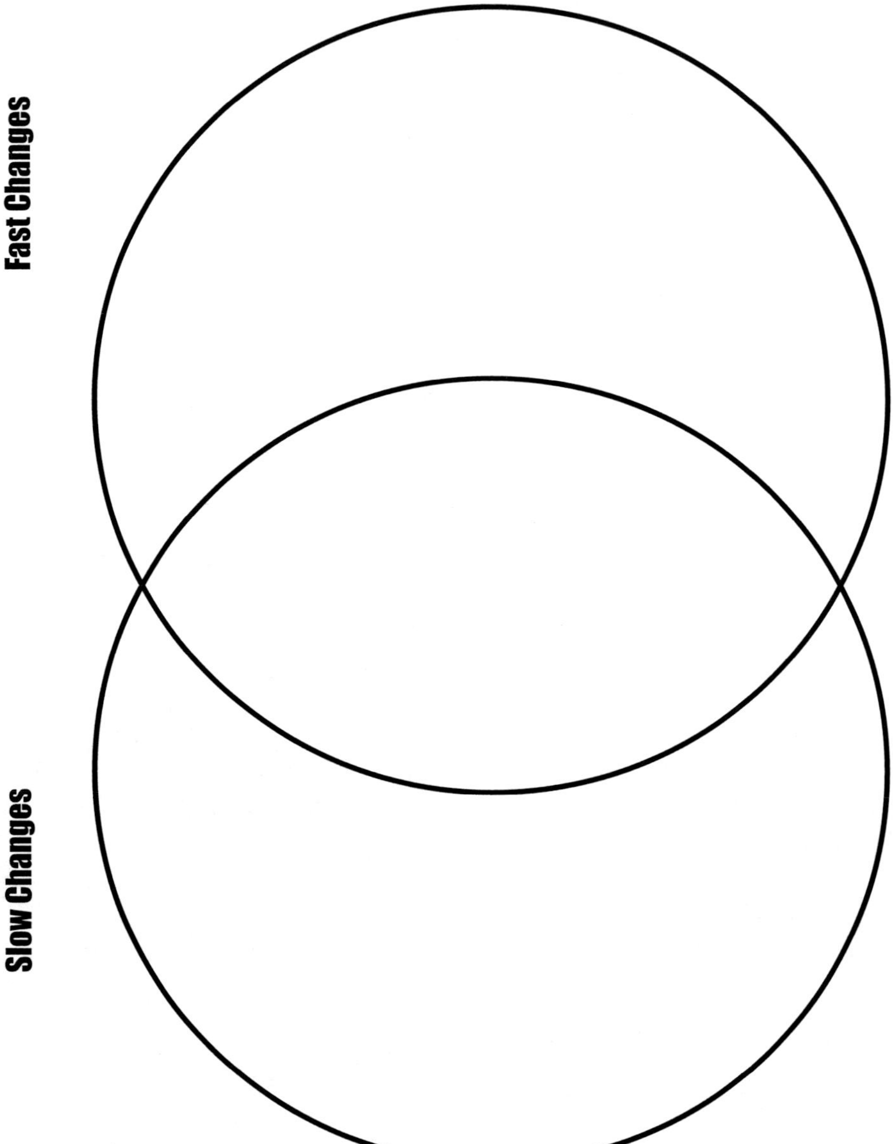

Mount St. Helens Blows Her Top

Read the text and answer the questions.

Outside Luke's bedroom window, the majestic Mount St. Helens towered over his family's cabin in the state of Washington. The mountain had been covered in thick clouds for what seemed like forever, but things were different this time. Luke peeked outside. Whoa! It wasn't the mountain he remembered—it was now a huge crater!

Luke knew an earthquake had struck Mount St. Helens a week earlier, on March 20, 1980. For the next few weeks, Luke watched Mount St. Helens rumble to life. Every day, ash and rock shot out of the mountain! A growing bulge on the side of the mountain was a sure sign that Mount St. Helens was ready to blow!

Luke was relieved when his family left the cabin in early May to stay with his grandmother in California for a while. It was too dangerous to stay! On May 18, 1980, Luke woke up to a dull booming sound, and he quickly turned on the television.

Mount St. Helens had erupted, and Luke had heard it all the way in California! A landslide raced down the mountain! Snow and ice turned instantly into gushing water! Hot ash and lava demolished everything! Luke knew his family had left just in time.

1. Summarize the 5 W's of this text.
   A. Who is the main character of this story?
   B. What event is occurring?
   C. When is the event occurring?
   D. Where is the event occurring?
   E. Why might an earthquake have caused Mt. St. Helens to "rumble to life?"
2. A. What words in the text help you "see" the action?
   B. What words in the text help you "feel" the action?
3. How is this event dangerous for humans?
4. Explain how volcanoes like Mt. St. Helens help to shape the history of the Earth.

The Rock Cycle

Read the text and answer the questions.

Geologists use rocks to study the Earth's history. Rocks hold clues to how the Earth was formed and the changes that have occurred over the many millions of years.

There are three types of rocks. Sedimentary rocks are formed from sediment on the Earth's surface (soil, pebbles, shells, and more) that has hardened over time. Igneous rocks are formed from magma or lava that has cooled and hardened. Metamorphic rocks are sedimentary or igneous rocks that become completely changed by intense pressure and heat from under the Earth's surface.

Some rocks on Earth are very old and have not changed much in millions of years. Other rocks are recently formed by volcanic activity or by heat and pressure inside the Earth's crust. New rocks on Earth are continuously being created from old rocks in a process called the rock cycle. As a rock goes through the rock cycle, it is slowly changed by weathering, erosion, heat, and pressure.

Geologists study this cycle to understand when and where a rock was created. For example, by studying the make-up of the soil around a volcano, geologists can determine when an eruption occurred and how old the rocks are in each layer of rock or soil around the volcano.

1. What is one characteristic used to distinguish between sedimentary, igneous, and metamorphic rock?
   a) color b) weight c) how it formed d) value
2. A. Where might you most likely find a sedimentary rock?
   B. Where might you most likely find an igneous rock?
   C. Where might you most likely find a metamorphic rock?
3. A. Use the text to define rock cycle.
   B. Why is the rock cycle important to the history of the Earth?
4. With a partner, choose one of the three types of rock. Use an online resource to research how it is formed and what rocks belong in that category. Create a digital presentation to share the information and include visuals. Give your presentation to the class.

MAIN IDEA

Comparing Layers

Read the text and answer the questions.

Sedimentary rock forms when Earth's surface rocks are broken down into smaller and smaller pieces by weathering and erosion. These small pieces of rock, sand, and minerals form a layer of loose rocky material called sediment. The remains of dead plants and animals are also mixed into the sediment. Over many millions of years, the sediment becomes a thicker and thicker layer. As more rock particles pile on top of the sediment, the layer is pushed down and compacted by the pressure of the sediment above. Over time, the sediment, made of tiny rock particles, is forced into becoming a solid layer of rock—sedimentary rock is formed!

Each layer of sedimentary rock that forms is slightly different than the ones above and below it. The type of sedimentary rock in a layer tells geologists about what the climate was like during that time, what plants and animals lived then, and even what geographic features the area had. Geologists know what animals and plants lived in each part of the Earth's history by studying fossils found in layers of sedimentary rock. By comparing similar layers of rock from around the world, geologists have constructed a history of the Earth.

Match each of the following questions to whether they are best answered by paragraph 1 or 2 of the text.

A. _____ Why do scientists compare different layers of rocks?
B. _____ How does sedimentary rock form?
C. _____ How do geologists know what types of life existed in the past?
D. _____ What forms sediment?

2. What roles do weathering and erosion play in the formation of sedimentary rock?

3. Why is sedimentary rock so important to understanding the history of the Earth?

4. What evidence in sedimentary rock describes the types of plant and animal life on Earth?

Law of Superposition

Read the text and answer the questions.

In the 1600s, many people became interested in science and began learning about the natural world around them. One of these people was Nicolaus Steno, a Danish priest who lived from 1636 to 1686, and studied anatomy and geology.

While working in the mountains of Italy, Steno noticed that he could sometimes see exposed layers, or strata, of sedimentary rock in the mountains. He observed that each layer of rock, or stratum, looked younger than the layer below it. Steno realized that, as long as the sedimentary rock was not disturbed in some way, younger layers of sediment always formed over older layers. This became known as the Law of Superposition.

Using the Law of Superposition and more observations of the natural world, Steno's work led to a total of four laws of stratigraphy, the study of rock layers. Geologists realized that these layers of sediment told the story of Earth's history in simple layers. The deeper into the Earth's crust geologists dug, the farther back in history they went.

PART A: Use the text to answer the questions.

1. A. What is the relationship between strata and stratigraphy?
   B. Stratum is the singular word for a rock layer. What is the plural?
   C. Who could be considered the "father of stratigraphy"?

2. A. Describe the Law of Superposition in your own words.
   B. Why is the Law of Superposition important to understanding Earth's history?

3. What effect did Steno's observations have on how geologists and other people viewed the Earth?

4. How might a volcano, earthquake, or other Earth process disturb the natural strata of sedimentary rock?

PART B: Match each of Steno's four laws to the diagram that best illustrates it.

Steno's Four Laws of Stratigraphy

1. **Law of Superposition**: Younger layers of rocks sit on top of older layers.

2. **Law of Original Horizontality**: Sedimentary rock layers are originally formed flat (horizontal).

3. **Law of Cross-Cutting Relationships**: Rock layers must be older than intrusions, like faults or magma, that disturb them.

4. **Law of Lateral Continuity**: Rock layers are continuous until something blocks their formation or until something acts upon rock layers that have already formed.

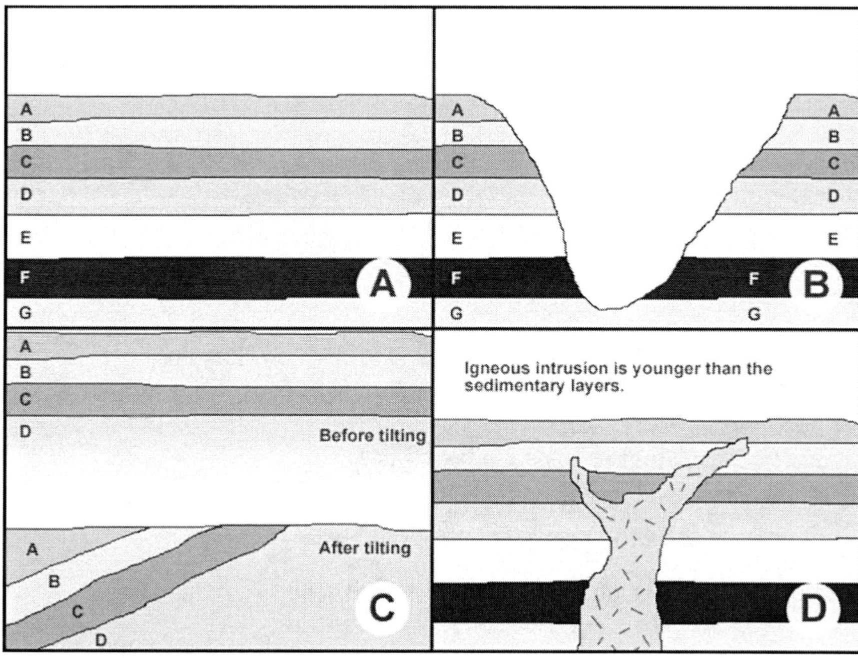

5. ______ Law of Cross-Cutting Relationships

6. ______ Law of Superposition

7. ______ Law of Lateral Continuity

8. ______ Law of Original Horizontality

What Are Fossils?

Read the text and answer the questions.

Fossils are the remains, usually found in rock, of things that lived long ago. Most fossils are formed when organisms, plants or animals, die and become buried. As the sediment builds up over the years, pressure turns the sediment into rock and the trapped remains of plants and animals into fossils.

There are two basic types of fossils. Body fossils show what an organism looked like when it was alive. Trace fossils show something an animal left behind when it was alive. Fossils can also be classified by how they were formed. Actual remains are dead, but completely preserved, organisms, usually found in tar, amber, or ice. Mold fossils are imprints left by organisms in sediment; once the sediment hardens into rock, the imprint becomes permanent. Cast fossils form when minerals fill in the imprints left by organisms.

All fossils show us the many kinds of plant and animal life that has existed on Earth. Through fossils, scientists learn how and when the organisms lived, and how they have changed over time.

1. A. Use the text to define fossil.
   B. Where might you find a fossil?

2. Match each of the following questions to whether they are best answered by paragraph 1, 2, or 3 of the text. Then answer each question.
   A. _____ What are the different types of fossils?
   B. _____ What are fossils and how are they made?
   C. _____ What do fossils tell us about Earth's history?

3. Use the text to complete the table by classifying each fossil.

Fossil	Body or Trace?	Remains, mold, or cast?
Dinosaur footprint in rock		
Prehistoric insect in amber		
Rock imprint of fern		
Mastodon frozen in glacier		

Fossils in the Valley

Read the text, examine the diagram, and answer the questions.

According to the Law of Superposition, older layers of rock are trapped below the younger layers of rock above them. Plants and animals that are buried in each layer become fossils.

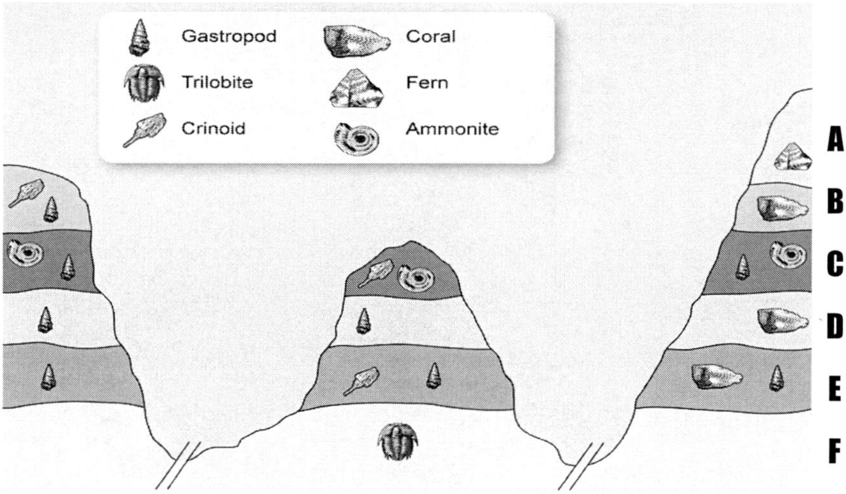

1. A. Which layer of rock is the oldest?
   B. Which layer of rock is the youngest?
2. What information can you gather about the history of the Earth from fossils in these layers?
3. Use the illustration to number the organisms in the order in which they first appeared in the Earth's history.

   a. _____ ammonite b _____ gastropod

   c. _____ trilobite d. _____ fern

4. ___"Extinct" means to no longer exist.
   A. Which organism from the diagram can you infer went extinct?
   B. What evidence from the diagram supports your answer?

CLASSIFYING INFORMATION

Geological Time Scale

Read the text, look at the diagram, and answer the questions in Parts A and B.

Since the Earth changes at such a slow rate, geologists need to measure time on a very large scale. They use the Geological Time Scale (GTS). Instead of measuring time in hours, days, months, and years, the GTS uses measurements of ages, epochs, periods, eras, and eons.

Age: millions of years

Epoch: tens of millions of years, spans several ages

Period: basic unit of the GTS, spans several epochs

Era: several hundred millions of years, spans several periods

Eon: half a billion years or more, spans several eras

Ma = million years ago

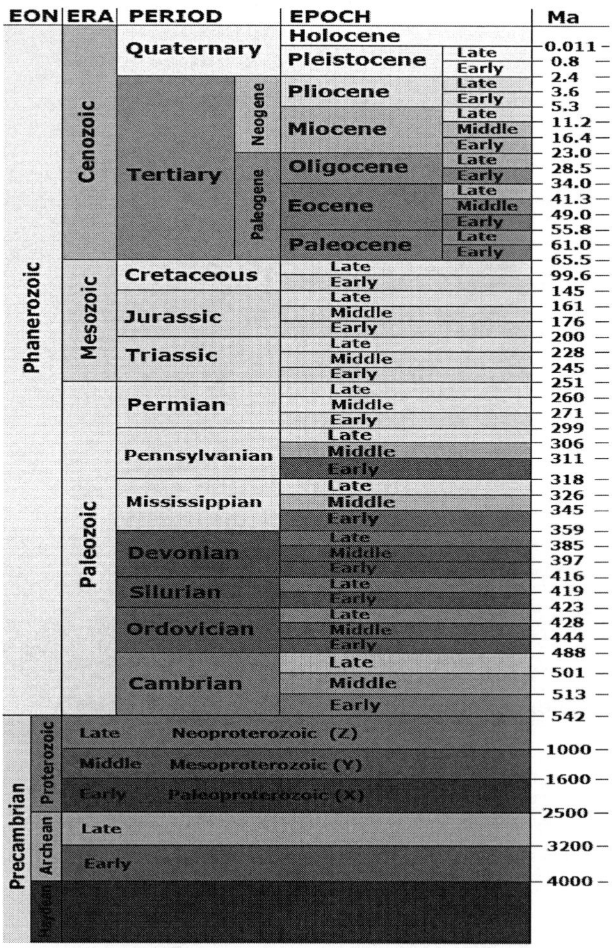

PART A: Use the geological time scale to answer the questions.

1. A. What is the Geological Time Scale?
   B. Why do geologists divide the Earth's history into smaller sections of time?

2. What unit is used to measure years on the Geological Time Scale?

Use information from the diagram to determine whether each answer is **true** (**T**) or **false** (**F**). Rewrite each false statement to be true.

A. _____ Eons, eras, periods, epochs, and ages are all units of time on the Geological Time Scale

B. _____ Geologists divide the Earth's history into large sections of time and then divide it into smaller sections of time.

C. _____ The Phanerozoic Era began about 100 million years ago.

D. _____ Ages are usually categorized as "early, middle, and late."

PART B: Look at the diagram and answer the questions.

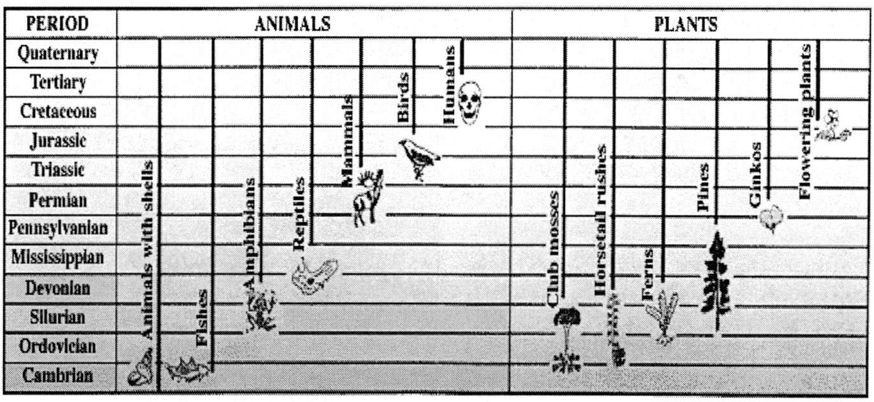

3. What unit of geological time is used in the diagram? Why?

4. Use the diagram to place the appearance of the listed plants and animals in chronological order, from 1 (earliest) to 13 (most recent).

A. _____ ferns
B. _____ humans
C. _____ birds
D. _____ ginkos
E. _____ mammals
F. _____ reptiles
G _____ pines
H. _____ horsetail rushes
I. _____ amphibians
J. _____ flowering plants
K. _____ animals with shells
L. _____ fishes
M. _____ club mosses

Earth's Timeline

The Geological Time Scale is used by geologists and other scientists to show major time periods of Earth's history.

ca. = circa (estimated time), because there are no exact dates
Ga = billion years ago
Ma = million years ago

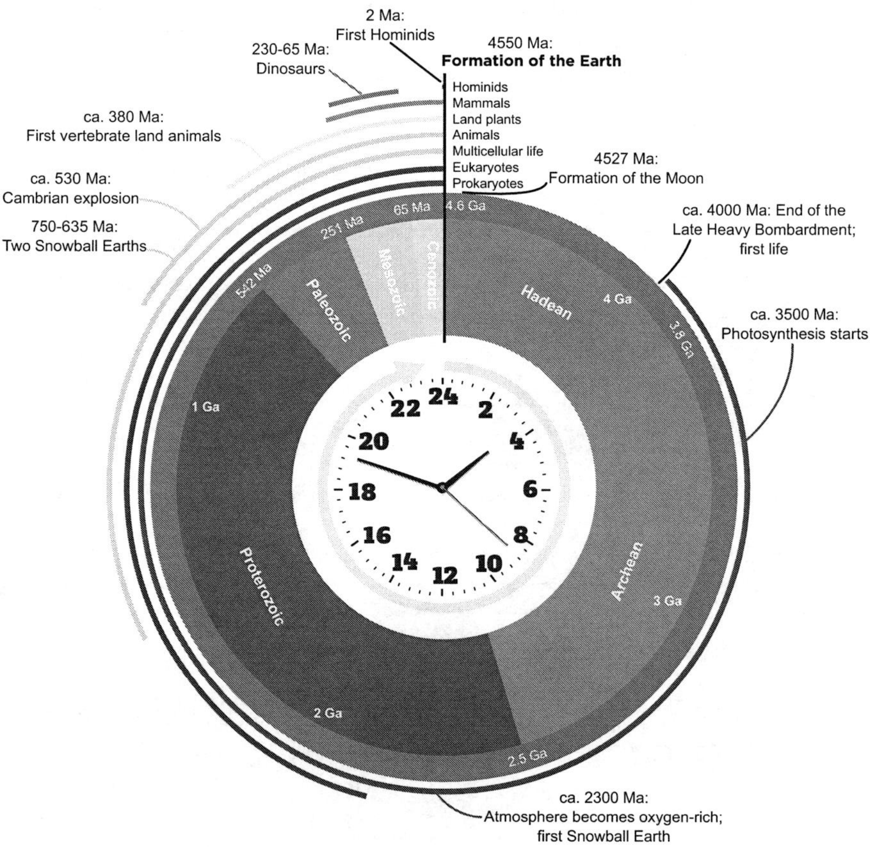

PART A: Examine the diagram and answer the questions.

1. Describe the shape and structure of this timeline.
   A. Where does the timeline begin?
   B. Where does the timeline end?

2. Arrange the time periods in the correct order, earliest (1) to most recent (6).

A.	_____ Paleozoic	D.	_____ Hadean
B.	_____ Archean	E.	_____ Proterozoic
C.	_____ Cenozoic	F.	_____ Mesozoic

PART B: Identify the period(s) on the timeline where the events occurred.

3. ______________________ Photosynthesis starts
4. ______________________ Multicellular life exists
5. ______________________ Moon forms
6. ______________________ Dinosaurs exist
7. ______________________ Atmosphere fills with oxygen
8. ______________________ Mammals develop

PART C: Use the diagram and text to answer the questions.

9. Geologists use Ga (giga-annum) and Ma (mega-annum) as abbreviations for the duration of time. Ga is a billion years ago and Ma is a million years ago. Infer what ka (kilo-annum) stands for.

10. Does presenting the timeline in a circle make it easier or more difficult to visualize and understand? Explain why.

11. The imaginary clock at the center of the diagram represents the Earth's history as a period of 24 hours or "1 day." Think about the periods of the Earth's history as if they are hours or minutes on this 24-hour clock.
    A. How many "hours" have animals existed on Earth??
    B. How many "hours" have mammals existed on Earth?
    C. Estimate how long humans have existed on Earth.

Long-Term Perspective

Read the text and answer the questions.

> *"...Our place in the history of the Earth reminds us that [humans have] occupied the planet for the tiniest fraction of that planet's four and a half thousand million years of existence...As we peer back through the fossil record, through layer upon layer of long-extinct species, many of which thrived far longer than the human species is ever likely to do, we are reminded of our mortality as a species. There is no law that declares [humans] to be different... from any other animal. There is no law that declares the human species to be immortal."* —Richard E. Leakey

1. A. Identify and list key words that you need to know to fully understand the passage.
   B. Use a dictionary or online resource to define the words.
2. The words mortality and immortal are best described as:
   a) homonyms b) homophones c) synonyms d) antonyms
3. Summarize the author's point of view about the history of the Earth.
4. What is the author's opinion about the future of the human race on Earth?
5. Mark which statements agree (A) and which statements disagree (D) with the quotation's point of view.
   A. _____ Human beings will be around until the end of time.
   B. _____ All species have a beginning and an end.
   C. _____ The laws of nature apply to human beings, just as they apply to every other living thing.
   D. _____ Humans have the special knowledge and skills that will help people survive for a long time on the Earth.
   E. _____ Humans are different than all other species on Earth.
   F. _____ Many species that are now extinct existed much longer than humans have.

Climate Changes

Read the text and answer the questions.

It is difficult to imagine that the Earth changes temperature, but in fact, the Earth has had several different climates throughout its history.

An Ice Age is a geological period of time during which much of the Earth is covered by sheets of ice, called glaciers. About 20,000 years ago, much of North America was buried under sheets of ice. This truth might be hard to believe, but scientists have found the evidence of glacial erosion all across North America.

Presently, the Earth is in a warm period. There are still glaciers in the far northern and far southern regions of the Earth. However, most of the Earth is covered by liquid water and dry land.

Throughout its history, the Earth has experienced many dramatic climate changes. Sometimes the climate has been hotter, sometimes colder, sometimes milder, and sometimes stormier. By studying rocks deep in the Earth, geologists are able to learn about the climates of different periods. Fossils show that climate greatly influences life on the planet. Some plants and animals need cold climates to survive, while others need very warm climates.

1. What is the main idea of this text?
2. Determine whether each statement is **true (T)** or **false (F)**.
   A. _____ When it is cold in the winter, it is called an Ice Age.
   B. _____ An Ice Age can last for thousands of years.
   C. _____ Before recently, the Earth was always covered in ice.
   D. _____ The Earth's climate changes throughout its history.
3. What evidence suggests that North America was once covered by a large sheet of glacial ice?
4. How might fossilized plant and animal remains give scientists clues about what climates existed at different points in Earth's history?
5. Infer whether the Earth's climate will stay the same or continue to fluctuate in the future. Support your answer with logical reasoning.

Plate Tectonics

The surface of the Earth is not one solid sheet of rock. The Earth's crust is actually made up of about 20 tectonic plates that sit on top of the mantle. There are seven or eight major plates, and many minor ones. The plates all fit together like a jigsaw puzzle.

Unlike the pieces of a jigsaw puzzle, the Earth's tectonic plates move. The plates float over the mantle like rafts on a lake. All the plates travel in different directions and at different speeds. This movement is called continental drift.

Generally, plates move slowly, at about the same rate as the growth of your fingernail. Even though plate movements are slow, they still cause dramatic changes. Mountains and trenches can take thousands of years to form. Sometimes, however, energy builds up and then releases suddenly, causing fast changes like earthquakes and tsunamis (large underwater waves).

A lot happens at the cracks in the Earth's crust where the plates meet. Those cracks are called faults. The plates rub and grind against one another along the fault lines. When two plates push together, the earth folds upward to form mountain ranges and volcanoes. When two plates pull away from each other, they can create new sea floors and underwater mountain ranges. When one plate slides under another, deep trenches can occur, the earth can fold and break, or even produce volcanoes. Some plates simply rub against each other, causing the plates to occasionally shift and slide—this sudden movement is what causes many earthquakes.

PART A: Use the text to answer the questions.

1. A. Define tectonic plates.
   B. Tectonic comes from the Greek "to build." Explain why tectonic plates are described as the building blocks of the Earth's crust.
2. What is the relationship between the Earth's crust and mantle?
3. What is continental drift? What causes it?
4. A simile is a comparison using "like" or "as."
   A. List two similes used in the text.
   B. Do they help you understand tectonic plates? Why or why not?

5. Cite evidence from the text to support the statement: "Tectonic plate movement causes both slow and fast changes to the Earth."

6. A. List at least five effects of plate tectonics.
   B. What effects of tectonic plate movement are invisible? Explain.
   C. What effects of tectonic plate movement can be seen or felt? Explain.
   D. Which effects could be potentially dangerous to people? Explain your answer and cite evidence from the text.

PART B: Look at the map and answer the questions.

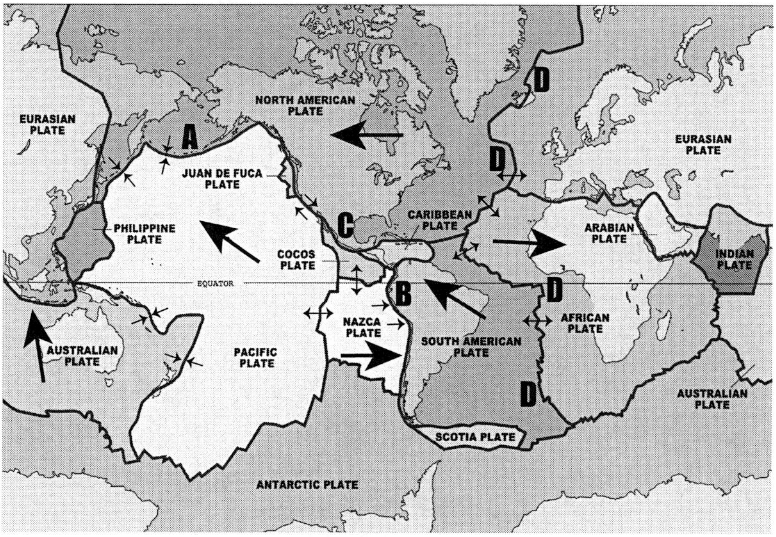

7. A. What does this map show about the Earth's crust?
   B. What do the large arrows on each plate show?
   C. What do the smaller arrows near plate boundaries show?

8. Use what you know about plate tectonics to explain how the group of islands marked A most likely formed.

9. What landforms might be found on the west coast of South America marked B?

10. A fault line marked C runs along the west coast of North America. Describe the movement of the two plates that caused this fault line.

11. The mid-Atlantic ridge is an underwater ridge marked by D. What tectonic plate process most likely created this ridge? Cite evidence from the text and map to support your answer.

Think Like a Geologist

For many hundreds of years, geologists and other scientists have wondered how the continents came to be in their present locations. The current answer to the question is the <u>Pangaea Theory</u>. Pangaea is a Greek word that means "whole Earth."

In the late 1500s, Abraham Ortelius, a Dutch mapmaker noticed that the coasts of some of the continents looked as if they fit together like pieces of a jigsaw puzzle, especially the coasts of Africa and South America. He hypothesized that the continents had once been part of one large landmass, or supercontinent, that was torn apart by earthquakes and floods.

In 1912, a German meteorologist, Alfred Wegener, changed the hypothesis. He thought that the supercontinent, named Pangaea, was actually broken apart over many millions of years by continental drift, the slow but constant movement of tectonic plates.

Wegener's research showed that not only do the continental coasts look like they fit together, all the continents have fossils from the ancient past of the same organisms. It seemed that life on Pangaea developed and spread across the supercontinent, and then traveled with the individual continents as they drifted apart.

Once the continents were separated, the fossil records show that organisms began to develop differently on each continent. Today, there is much <u>biodiversity</u>, or variety of life, between the plants and animals that live on different continents. For example, giraffes and elephants naturally live in Africa, but not in North America.

PART A: Make inferences from information in the text to answer the questions.

1. A. Summarize the <u>Pangaea Theory</u>.
   B. What inspired Ortelius to come up with his hypothesis?
   C. Describe the change that Wegener made to Ortelius' hypothesis.
2. Why are fossils of certain organisms found on all the continents?
3. The word Pangaea is made from *Pan* = *entire*, and *Gaia* = *Earth*. When Pangaea existed, the Earth also had one large body of ocean water, Panthalassa. Infer the meaning of "thalassa."

4. A. Explain the meaning of the word biodiversity.
   B. Infer why biodiversity occurs in different continents.

5. Write a paragraph of your own theory of why the continents are in their present locations, and how ancient fossil records show that the same organisms lived on all the continents in the past.

PART B: Read the text and answer the questions.

Scientists use the Scientific Method to help them logically answer questions about the natural world. The Scientific Method starts with a **question**. After asking the question, scientists do **research** to learn about the subject, and come up with a possible answer to the question, called a **hypothesis**.

Scientists then design an **experiment** to test the truth of the hypothesis. Once testing is done, the results are reviewed in a step called **analysis**. If the analysis shows the hypothesis is correct, the question has an answer. If it is not correct, scientists develop another hypothesis and try again. Either way, scientists always **report** what has happened so everyone can learn from their experiences.

6. What is the purpose of the Scientific Method?

7. A. List the steps of the scientific method in order in the first column.
   B. In the second column, explain how Wegner used each step of the Scientific Method to develop the Pangaea Theory.

Scientific Method Steps	Alfred Wegner

Correlations to Common Core State Standards

For your convenience, correlations are listed page-by-page, and for the entire book!

This book is correlated to the Common Core State Standards for English Language Arts grades 3-8, and to Common Core State Standards for Literacy in History, Science, & Technological Subjects grades 6-8.

Correlations are highlighted in gray.

PAGE #	READING *Includes:* RI: Reading Informational Text RST: Reading Science & Technical Subjects	WRITING *Includes:* W: Writing WHST: Writing History/Social Studies, Science, & Technical Subjects	LANGUAGE *Includes:* L: Language LF: Language Foundational Skills	SPEAKING & LISTENING *Includes:* SL: Speaking & Listening
2	RI RST . **1 2 3 4 5** 6 7 **8** 9 **10**	W WHST . 1 **2** 3 **4** 5 6 7 **8 9 10**	L LF . 1 2 3 **4 5 6**	SL . 1 2 3 4 5 6
3	RI RST . **1 2 3 4** 5 6 **7** 8 **9 10**	W WHST . 1 **2** 3 **4** 5 6 7 **8 9 10**	L LF . 1 2 3 **4 5 6**	SL . 1 2 3 4 5 6
4-5	RI RST . **1 2 3 4 5 6** 7 **8 9 10**	W WHST . **1 2 3 4** 5 6 7 8 **9 10**	L LF . 1 2 3 **4 5 6**	SL . 1 2 3 4 5 6
6	RI RST . **1** 2 3 4 **5** 6 7 8 **9 10**	W WHST . 1 2 3 4 5 6 7 8 9 10	L LF . 1 2 **3** 4 5 **6**	SL . 1 2 3 4 5 6
7	RI RST . **1 2** 3 **4 5** 6 7 **8** 9 **10**	W WHST . 1 **2** 3 **4** 5 6 7 8 **9 10**	L LF . 1 2 3 **4** 5 **6**	SL . 1 2 3 4 5 6
8	RI RST . **1 2 3 4 5** 6 7 8 **9 10**	W WHST . 1 **2** 3 **4 5 6 7 8 9 10**	L LF . 1 2 3 **4** 5 **6**	SL . **1** 2 3 **4 5 6**
9	RI RST . **1 2 3** 4 **5** 6 7 **8** 9 **10**	W WHST . 1 **2** 3 **4** 5 6 7 8 **9 10**	L LF . 1 2 3 4 5 6	SL . 1 2 3 4 5 6
10-11	RI RST . **1 2 3 4 5 6** 7 8 **9 10**	W WHST . 1 **2** 3 **4** 5 6 7 **8 9 10**	L LF . 1 2 3 **4 5 6**	SL . 1 2 3 4 5 6
12	RI RST . **1 2 3 4 5** 6 7 **8** 9 **10**	W WHST . 1 **2** 3 **4** 5 6 7 8 **9 10**	L LF . 1 2 3 **4** 5 **6**	SL . 1 2 3 4 5 6
13	RI RST . **1 2 3 4 5** 6 **7** 8 **9 10**	W WHST . 1 **2** 3 **4** 5 6 7 **8 9 10**	L LF . 1 2 3 **4** 5 **6**	SL . 1 2 3 4 5 6
14-15	RI RST . **1 2 3 4 5 6 7** 8 **9 10**	W WHST . 1 **2** 3 **4** 5 6 7 **8** 9 **10**	L LF . 1 2 3 **4 5 6**	SL . 1 2 3 4 5 6
16-17	RI RST . **1 2 3 4 5** 6 **7** 8 9 **10**	W WHST . 1 **2** 3 **4** 5 6 7 **8 9 10**	L LF . 1 2 3 **4** 5 6	SL . **1** 2 3 4 5 6
18	RI RST . **1 2 3 4 5 6** 7 **8** 9 **10**	W WHST . **1 2** 3 **4** 5 6 7 8 **9 10**	L LF . 1 2 **3 4 5 6**	SL . 1 2 3 4 5 6
19	RI RST . **1 2 3** 4 **5** 6 7 **8** 9 **10**	W WHST . **1 2** 3 **4** 5 6 7 **8 9 10**	L LF . 1 2 3 4 5 6	SL . 1 2 3 4 5 6
20-21	RI RST . **1 2 3 4 5** 6 **7 8 9 10**	W WHST . 1 **2** 3 **4** 5 6 7 **8** 9 **10**	L LF . 1 2 3 **4 5 6**	SL . 1 2 3 4 5 6
22-23	RI RST . **1 2 3 4 5** 6 7 **8 9 10**	W WHST . 1 **2** 3 **4 5** 6 **7 8 9 10**	L LF . 1 2 **3 4 5 6**	SL . 1 2 3 4 5 6
COMPLETE BOOK	RI RST . **1 2 3 4 5 6 7 8 9 10**	W WHST . **1 2 3 4 5 6 7 8 9 10**	L LF . 1 2 **3 4 5 6**	SL . **1** 2 3 **4 5 6**

For the complete Common Core standard identifier, combine your grade + "." + letter code above + "." + number code above.

In addition to the correlations indicated here, the activities may be adapted or expanded to align to additional standards and to meet the diverse needs of your unique students!